done.

what most religions
never tell you

SECOND EDITION

Cary Schmidt

Copyright © 2024 by In the Gospel Publishing.
All Scripture quotations are taken from
the King James Version.

First published in 2005. Second Edition published in 2024.

All rights reserved. No part of this book may be reproduced, stored in a retrieval system, or transmitted in any form or by any means—electronic, mechanical, photocopy, recording, or otherwise—without written permission of the publisher, except for brief quotations in printed reviews.

In the Gospel Publishing
2875 W Ray Rd Suite 6-346
Chandler, AZ 85224
800.201.7748
inthegospel.com

Cover design by Lance Schmidt and Craig Parker
Layout by Craig Parker
Editing, proofreading, and assistance by Ashlee Dickerson

ISBN 979-8-9891866-0-0

Printed in the United States of America

Table of Contents

Introduction v

ONE — More Than a Body 1

TWO — The Only Two Religions in the World. 9

THREE — Knowing Where You're Going. 23

FOUR — Birth Defect. 29

FIVE — God's Only Accepted Method of Payment 39

SIX — Can I Get a Substitute? 51

SEVEN — God's Only Miraculous Substitute. 57

EIGHT — Paid in Full 65

NINE — The Greatest Gift. 75

TEN — Believing on Christ 83

CONCLUSION — New Creature,
                         New Life, New Future. 97

Introduction

If God were willing to sit down with you personally and allow you to air your questions, reason through your doubts, and pose any challenge—would you take Him up on His offer? Would you be *willing* to investigate His claims and understand His purposes? Would you be willing to believe Him?

Friend, He has extended just such an invitation to you. In Isaiah 1:18 God personally says, *"Come now, let us reason together."* God isn't intimidated by your questions and isn't surprised by your doubts. In fact, quite the opposite is true. He is fully aware of every detail of your life, and still, He invites you to approach

Him personally and reason with Him through your life's questions.

I invite you to do just that through this short book. Find a quiet place, open your heart, and consider the message of God's word—a message that is diluted, distorted, and even perverted by man-made religious systems, but is simple and powerful to the human heart.

You see, there's an amazing message in the Bible, one of astonishing good news with incredible implications for your life, yet you won't find it in the pulpits of most churches or in the pages of most religious books. It's a message understandable to a little child but missed by so many full-grown adults. It's a message that is verifiable by intelligent reason but only receivable by simple faith.

Honestly, it could change your life *forever*.

It's the most important message you will ever consider. It's literally life and death.

Could you spare a few minutes to understand this message?

I don't know where this little book finds you or how it came to you, but I don't believe it's an accident. Perhaps you are searching for some answers about life. Perhaps you're cynical of organized religion but somewhat curious about truth and God.

Introduction

By now, you know there's more to this life than just time, and you know in your heart that you are more than just a body! There must be a *purpose*—a reason for it all. There must be hope. There must be more than just birth, life, death, and an endless evolutionary cycle randomly headed nowhere. You must be more valuable than that, and your future must mean more than that!

Deep within, you *know* these things because they are written in your heart—etched into your conscience—like a deeply woven thread, impossible to remove. These truths are a part of your spiritual genetics. You know you were created because your world shows intelligent design. You know your Creator must be good because He created so many good things. Yet, you live in a world with pain, problems, questions, and doubts. We live in a world where God has given us enough information to know He exists, but deep within, we all long for more. We *know* there's more, and God promises to give us more if we choose to seek Him.

Are you willing for a moment to investigate and consider the possibility that God truly does exist and that He cares about you? Are you willing to see reliable evidence and consider what it might mean for your life?

What if your conclusions about life, death, and eternity are established on faulty information? What if the version of God or Jesus that you rejected is a false version? What if there's more you were never told?

Suppose for a moment that there truly is a God. Suppose that He created you and loves you intensely. Imagine that He has a perfect, eternal purpose for you, but that you are now held hostage by a ruthless enemy, whom you cannot see, and who is bent on destroying you. Imagine that this loving God is on a rescue mission to save you, and this is all going on behind the scenes of your life—behind the visible wall of your day-to-day existence. Unseen but deeply felt. Perhaps you've never given it a moment's thought, and now it's time to think more deeply.

If you could know with certainty where you would spend eternity—if you could forever put away every fear you've ever had—if this incredible, loving God was knocking at your door right now, offering to rescue you from it all, would you let Him in? Would you even give Him a chance?

Wouldn't you want to know this God?

If being loved by God matters to you, then all I ask is that you give Him a chance to connect with your heart through the pages of this book.

Keep reading—I think you're going to like this story!

CHAPTER ONE

More Than a Body

He sat across the table from me openly admitting that for the first time in his fifty years of life, he was searching. "In the last three years, I've gone from being an atheist to being a believer. I've come to the conclusion, with all the good and bad in my life, that there's no reason I should have had it this good. I'm starting to believe in God."

He was the manager of a restaurant I liked to visit, and one day I felt impressed in my heart to introduce him to the message you hold in your hand. This was our third conversation together, and for the first time in his life, he was seeing that there must be more to life than just the passing of time and a meaningless string of circumstances and events. He admitted to having questions and hoping that there was more to life that he didn't yet understand.

As our conversation ended, I politely asked him if I could continue addressing his questions and pursuing these topics with him. His answer? "Absolutely, so long as you don't mind me asking them!"

From there I promised to give him plenty of "food for thought," and I promised to support those thoughts with references from God's word so that he could verify them himself.

In the same spirit, I would ask you to consider this first important truth as we take this journey together.

You are more than a body!

Contrary to the message of pop culture, deep in your heart you know that there is more to you than just flesh, blood, and randomly evolved biological substances. There is much more to you than what you shave, shower, and dress every morning!

Jesus said it way, *"The life is more than meat, and the body is more than raiment"* (Luke 12:23). Again, God said in His Word, *"I pray God your whole spirit and soul and body be preserved blameless unto the coming of our Lord Jesus Christ"* (1 Thessalonians 5:23).

Chapter One—More Than a Body

In James 2:26 God says, *"the body without the spirit is dead."* In 2 Corinthians 4:16, God distinguishes between the "outer man" (our body) and the "inward man" (our soul and spirit): *"though our outward man perish, yet the inward man is renewed day by day."*

More than a body—why is this so important?

Well, first, this means you have a *future*! It means you have more than only death to anticipate. Think about it. If you're nothing but a body, then all you really have to look forward to is death. How could anybody really be happy if that's all the future holds? If that is to be the ultimate and final destination of your life, why would anything else matter much at all?

Second, it means you have *value*. If you are more than a freak biological accident, then you are created. If you are created, then you have value to your Creator. He made you for a reason—a purpose. You have significance and meaning—and life is more than random events strung together by fate or chance.

Third, it means you have *hope*. There's more than just physical life and death. There's hope that you can get past your present difficulties and someday enter something far better.

Ever heard that little phrase "Life's hard, then you die"? Well, that's a pretty hopeless outlook on life, and it's definitely not what God clearly says. Yes, life is sometimes very hard and very unpredictable. Yes, everyone eventually dies. But in God's good news to you, there's more to it! There's more to life than what you can see and more to your story than just time itself.

Do you want proof? Okay. *Conscience.*

You have a conscience.

Here's what I mean. How can biological matter spontaneously develop a conscience? That's like saying I can hurt my refrigerator's feelings! Conscience is a soul thing, a spiritual thing, and meat doesn't generate spiritual events. Meat is just meat—it doesn't feel good or bad—it just sits there and rots once life has departed. I'm not trying to be crude, just clear.

Friend, your conscience proves your soul's existence. Conscience is your internal knowledge of right and wrong. Conscience is your God-given knowledge of your Creator and His moral standard in all of creation.

The fact that human beings all over planet Earth intuitively worship something is proof that God has written this in our hearts. It's a part of our spiritual genetics. No matter where you go, you will find every person worshipping someone or something. Everybody worships. Even the atheist who denies God's existence

Chapter One—More Than a Body

chooses to worship self, and self becomes god. We all give and live our lives to something or someone that is *ultimate*. That's worship. The question is this: is that something *truthfully ultimate* or will it only eventually prove insufficient to save us from death?

In Romans 1, God brings an indictment against men who deny what He has clearly written on their hearts and revealed in them.

He says in Romans 1:20, *"For the invisible things of him from the creation of the world are clearly seen, being understood by the things that are made, even his eternal power and Godhead; so that they are without excuse."* In verse 19 of that same chapter, God says that He has revealed Himself inside of every human being, and in verse 21 He explains that when we willfully choose to deny this inner knowledge, our hearts become darkened.

Once again, in Romans 2:15 He says that His law is written in our hearts: *"Which shew the work of the law written in their hearts, their conscience also bearing witness."*

What does all this mean? God says it quite simply in Romans 1:20. We are "without excuse."

To deny the existence of a Creator or His interest in our lives is to literally ignore our conscience and the truth that God has written in our hearts. When we deny Him, we begin a long walk in the dark, and life loses its meaning and hope.

This all points to one primary conclusion. Our relationship to God must be intentionally designed to function by faith rather than sight. God says it this way, *"Through faith we understand that the worlds were framed by the word of God, so that things which are seen were not made of things which do appear"* (Hebrews 11:3).

Things which are seen (that's you and me) were not made of things which do appear (that's the world around us). In other words, who you are, where you came from, and where you are going have more to do with what you *cannot* see than with what you *can* see.

You cannot see the wind, but you know it exists. You cannot see air, but you depend upon it for life. You cannot see hope, joy, or peace—but you desperately long for these in your heart. You cannot see God, but you know He exists and your heart longs to be loved and accepted fully by Him.

More than a body? You bet! Your body is just a temporary dwelling place for the real you. God even calls it a tent in 2 Corinthians 5:1! Just as you take off one set of clothes each night and put on another set the

Chapter One—More Than a Body

next morning, one day you will vacate your body. We call this death—the separation of your body and soul. Your inner self will vacate its tent. In that moment, your body will cease to breathe and move and function, but the real you, the inner you, will very much continue to live.

Yes, you are much more than a body! Take care of yours while you have it, but don't focus so much on the physical that you miss "what you cannot see with your eyes." You are a *soul*. You have a conscience. You are created and you matter. You have value. You have an eternal purpose. You have a Creator who longs for you to read the clues—to see with your heart what you cannot see with your eyes. He has given you plenty of information to put two and two together, and He is waiting for you to come to Him personally.

As we close this chapter, I have a short assignment for you. In Ephesians 1:18, there is a prayer that states the following: *"The eyes of your understanding being enlightened; that ye may know what is the hope of his calling."* In other words, you have a second set of eyes —the eyes of your understanding, and these eyes may or may not be functioning correctly.

Would you pray this simple prayer from a sincere heart to God before you continue reading? Even if you don't fully believe in Him yet, go ahead and give it a sincere whisper. I dare you.

"God, I understand and accept that I am more than a body and that perhaps there is much about the spiritual life that I do not see or understand. As I read about these things, would you open the eyes of my understanding and help me see what I am missing? I sincerely want to know the truth. Amen."

CHAPTER TWO

The Only Two Religions in the World

How many religions are there in the world?

Hundreds? Perhaps thousands? Just trying to comprehend all the various belief systems and religious structures in America alone can be mind-boggling. Most people have their fair share of confusion and frustration trying to figure out which religion believes what and in what ways they are different.

In fact, it seems that the latest craze is to just toss them all into the same category and say, "They're all the same. We're all going to the same place if we sincerely believe." While this thinking feels convenient, it doesn't really make sense. Let's be rational if nothing else.

What these religions believe from one to the next varies widely. In fact, some are diametrically opposed in belief. It sounds nice to conclude that "all roads lead to the same place" but that theory doesn't hold water, and it isn't supported by God's word.

So how do you sift through all the religious "fluff" and cut to the heart of the matter? How can you know truth from error—fact from fiction? How can you discern between God's true design and man's cheap substitutes? The answer to these questions is more simple than you could ever imagine.

Back to my original question. How many religions are there in the world?

Would you believe *two*?

The truth is, you can categorize every single religion in the world into one of two basic categories. You can strip away all externals, from minor differences to major theological divides, and cut right to the heart of the matter rather easily.

Think of it this way. Most religions agree on what we discussed in chapter 1. Most people acknowledge a Creator and a spiritual world. It's defining that Creator and understanding that spiritual world that starts to reveal the differences.

Chapter Two—The Only Two Religions in the World

More importantly, it's how to *know* the Creator and how to enter into a peaceful "afterlife" that really separates the groups. In other words, how do we reach God, and how do we get to Heaven? In some form or fashion, most religions of the world are attempting to answer these two basic questions.

So, how can we take so many complicated systems of belief and simplify them down to two basic belief systems?

Two words: DO or DONE. Remember those words, because by the end of this book, they will be very important!

First, let's look at the DO religions. These religions are, in truth, *systems* of religions. Their central message is "what you must DO to gain the approval of God and to earn entrance into Heaven."

The general agreement among these religions is that man is somehow separated from God and must DO something to be restored to Him. In these systems, God is like an upset substitute teacher, and He's very angry that people are misbehaving. He's somewhere up in Heaven, upset with the whole human race for doing things that displease Him, and He's expecting everyone to make up for their wrongs by DOING good things. He's sitting on His throne, arms folded, expecting humanity to compensate or atone for their failures by doing good deeds or religious things for Him.

Now, the *definition* of "what God wants us to DO" varies widely, and thus we have so many differing systems of belief, but the core—the essence—is still the same. The message is simply this, "DO." Do the right stuff, don't do the wrong stuff, and somehow God will grant you acceptance into Heaven.

It's like having the same macaroni and cheese cooked fifty-two different ways. The substance and central message of each of these religions are identical. "God is upset at you, so you'd better start doing good things to make Him happy!"

In this DO category, every religion has a different list of "DOs" and "DON'Ts." For some, the list is extremely long and tedious: confess your sins, get baptized, give money, get confirmed, shave your head, sell flowers at the airport, sell literature door to door, etc. The list is as endless as the imaginations of men and women. And with every passing decade new religions are popping up with new lists of stuff to do.

For other systems it's more basic and general: be good, be nice, and generally try to outweigh your bad works by your good works. Think about how nebulous that is, not to mention *risky*! How could you ever know

Chapter Two—The Only Two Religions in the World

if you've been good enough? How could you ever do enough? Who has the right list? You can already see how unloving and anxiety-inducing these man-made systems can be for the human heart.

Their foundation is fear, not love.

For some systems, the list is extreme and even bizarre: instituting rituals of self-mutilation, child sacrifice, suicide, murder, and painful forms of bondage or penance.

Either way, the basic intent and the central message is the same—you must *work* your way to God. You must perform God's list, DO God's demands, appease God's anger, and earn God's forgiveness. These systems are the ultimate form of religious bondage for millions of people all over the planet. They are held hostage to fear and are bound to intricate systems of religious behavior that they are convinced will restore them to God and give them eternal life.

The DO religions vary widely in style and structure (they come in many different cultures and flavors), but they all add up to performance-based acceptance —cheap love. God is the taskmaster and we humans are the slave labor. Essentially God refuses to love us until we DO things that make Him happy.

The saddest thing about these systems is that they offer only despair, bondage, fear, and anxiety. They leave the human heart feeling ultimately rejected by God and forever wondering, "Have I done enough?" They characterize God more as an oppressor than a heavenly Father, and they leave your heart feeling *anything but* close to God.

These systems fill the heart with nagging doubts. What if I missed something? What if I haven't lived up to God's demands? What if I'm doing the wrong list? What if my list is missing some critical element? Have I been good enough? How good is good enough? What if I haven't been good enough?

These systems are great for building wealthy, powerful religions because they enslave people to fear, but they do nothing to relieve the inner fears and yearnings of our hearts. They do nothing to heal the conscience and truly bring us into God's unconditional love and favor. They do nothing to introduce us personally to the loving heavenly Father that God says He is and that our hearts deeply long to know.

You see, the question we must ask when looking at these systems is "What has God said?" When it comes to being restored to God and gaining life with Him, what are His instructions?

Chapter Two—The Only Two Religions in the World

Very few people realize this, but to accept *any* of the DO religions, you must basically throw away the central message of God's word! Look at these Scriptures for yourself and consider what God is saying to you…

"Not by works of righteousness which we have done, but according to his mercy he saved us" (Titus 3:5). In other words, you cannot gain God's favor by doing good works.

Again, God says, *"Therefore by the deeds of the law there shall no flesh be justified in his sight: for by the law is the knowledge of sin"* (Romans 3:20). He's saying, "You cannot justify yourself in my sight by doing good deeds."

Here's another one, *"But to him that worketh not, but believeth on him that justifieth the ungodly, his faith is counted for righteousness"* (Romans 4:5). In that verse God literally says that you cannot do good works to gain God's favor.

How much more clearly can God say it than this, *"Knowing that a man is not justified by the works of the law"* (Galatians 2:16).

God goes on to say that His favor cannot be earned. He says in Ephesians 2:8–9 that salvation is *"not of yourselves: it is the gift of God: Not of works."* Think about that! "Not of works."

What does that mean?

Quite simply, there's not a DO list on the planet—there's not a religious system ever invented—that will gain you one bit of favor or love from God or bring you any closer to His presence.

Now I know what you're thinking. "How can this be? Surely, I can please God by doing good!" Hang in there. A good life is very meaningful, but remember we're talking about coming to God and relating to Him. We're talking about being *restored* to Him in relationships. We're not talking about all the fringe benefits of being honest, living a good life, and giving to charity.

We're asking this question: Does doing these things gain me any "brownie points" with God? If I do them, does He approve of me, accept me, forgive me, or love me more?

Most religions say, "Yes...so long as you are doing *our* list."

In God's own words to you, He says no. It is *"not by works of righteousness which we have done"* (Titus 3:5). Many times and in many ways God says, "You cannot earn your way to me. You cannot DO anything to gain my favor or to earn my acceptance." Perhaps one of the most hard-hitting ways He phrases it is in

Chapter Two—The Only Two Religions in the World

Isaiah 64:6, *"But we are all as an unclean thing, and all our righteousnesses are as filthy rags; and we all do fade as a leaf; and our iniquities, like the wind, have taken us away."*

In this verse, God is saying, "There is something so massively dividing us that even your *best* behavior is pointless." Good behavior is useless against the problem that divides us from God. We'll talk more about this later, but for now, you must understand that God never tells us that performance gains His salvation. His love cannot be earned, but thankfully it can be received. He desires to love you purely—unconditionally, which is also how we most deeply long to be loved.

The conclusion of the matter is this. "DO" doesn't cut it. Nowhere in the Bible is there even one verse that teaches that God accepts me more, loves me more, or forgives my sin when I DO the right things. Doing good works doesn't gain favor with God.

Why? Well, God isn't as concerned with how I *behave* as He is with who I *am*. He isn't as concerned about *ruling* me as He is with *relating* to me. He's not impressed with a cold religion. He wants a close relationship. I don't DO relationships. I DO my chores.

We'll get back to this thought in another chapter, but first, let's look at that other word—DONE.

Done

DONE. Finished. Complete. Full. Ended. Ready. Accomplished. Fulfilled. Perfected. What a great word!

Though most religions of the world fit into the DO category, there is still the DONE category!

The true message of the Bible is DONE. In other words, everything necessary to restore you to God and bring you into eternal life with Him has already been DONE.

When Jesus was hanging on the cross, He said these words, *"It is finished"* (John 19:30). The phrase literally means "paid in full." DONE.

Those were some of the last words He spoke before He died. At that moment, something amazing happened in Jerusalem. In the temple—a building symbolic of God's presence—there was a veil (or heavy curtain) separating the most sacred representation of God's presence from the outer visible areas. Common people were not permitted to go behind that curtain into God's presence. But at the moment that Jesus died, this veil was miraculously torn in half from top to bottom—thrown open for all.

The picture is this: suddenly, whatever separated God from man was now completely removed, and God was inviting all humankind to come directly to Him! It was God saying to the whole human race, "DONE!"

Chapter Two—The Only Two Religions in the World

You can now have access behind the curtain and directly into God's presence!

DONE says, "There's nothing more to do." The price is paid. The debt is forgiven. The atonement (or full payment) is complete. If you try to earn it, work for it, or DO something to get it, you're wasting your time. It's already DONE. Or in the words of Jesus on the cross, *"It is finished."*

Think of it this way. Imagine that you've prepared a wonderful Christmas morning for your family. You've saved, shopped, wrapped, decorated, and made all the preparations. On Christmas morning, imagine that your kids come running downstairs eager to celebrate Christmas, but rather than sitting down to open gifts, they begin feverishly doing things for you. They start cleaning the garage, washing the cars, doing the dishes, polishing your shoes, and whatever else they can find to do. Other than having a heart attack, you would probably be disappointed! You would stop them and ask, "What are you kids doing? This isn't the time for good works, this is the time for gift-giving!"

Suppose their response goes something like this, "Dad and Mom, we've realized that we don't deserve your gifts to us, and so we've decided to earn them—to pay for them by doing good works. We've decided to serve you and do things so that we can deserve or earn your kindness."

What would you do? You would probably explain that this is unnecessary! You would tell your kids how much trouble you've gone to in saving, shopping, and purchasing gifts. You don't want their service (at least not yet) so much as you just want to enjoy Christmas morning and present them with their gifts—your free expressions of love.

This is the message of God to humanity. "So long as you are busying yourself with DOING, you're missing what I've already DONE." The gift is purchased, the table is set, and there's no need to do anything more! All the preparations have been made. *"Come now, let us reason together."* His invitation to you is not to DO for Him, but rather to come to Him.

With all the religions in the world, are there really only two? That's the bottom line. Just two.

DO or DONE.

Here's another way to say it: religion or relationship. Does God institute *systems* that lead to Him, or does He desire something more personal—*relational*? Maybe the fact that He tells us to call Him Dad or Father should shed a little light on the situation. He wants a relationship with you. And close relationships

Chapter Two—The Only Two Religions in the World

are not a product of DOING, but rather a product of BEING or BELONGING.

Since you are more than a body and you have a Creator, what is the way to know that Creator? What are His answers to those two questions: How do I come to God, and how do I gain Heaven or "everlasting life" (as Jesus called it)? His answers in the Bible are clear.

You can't earn your way into eternal life. You can't DO anything to get there. You can't perform your way into God's presence. He wants more than an "employee/employer relationship." He wants more than cold religion. He wants a close relationship.

Most importantly, everything required to close the gap between you and God has already been DONE. There's nothing more you can DO to earn His favor or gain His salvation.

So, indeed there are just two religions in the world. DO and DONE. Are you stuck on DO? Are you trapped in a system of performance thinking you're headed in the right direction? Are you trying to earn your way to God?

I often ask people this question, "If you died today, would you go to Heaven?" Interestingly, most people say, "Yes, I think I would." When I ask "Why?" they answer something like this, "Because I'm trying to be a good person, and I've tried to do good things."

You know what they are saying? I'm DOING. Friend, are you stuck on DOING? If so, you're missing the central message of God's word. If you're trusting a performance-based system of religion, you're missing God's true way of coming to Him.

What would you say to that question? What are you trusting? DO or DONE? Do you have a religion or do you have a relationship?

Hey, thanks for hanging with me for this long. We're twenty-two pages in, and we have about eighty more to go. By now you know that you're more than a body and that God's guidelines for knowing Him do not involve DOING.

Let's press on. The next chapter has some pretty good news you've probably never heard.

CHAPTER THREE

Knowing Where You're Going

Understanding the fact that we are more than a body leaves us with a nagging question. *Where does the rest of me go when my body dies?*

Do we just "hang around" planet Earth haunting people? Are we reincarnated into another life form? Do we go to purgatory and try to continue earning our way to a blissful afterlife?

Everybody has an opinion, but opinions aren't the kind of thing on which you stake your eternal destination. Once again, we must turn to God's word for answers to these questions and see what God actually says. Yes, His word does say that the real you will live on somewhere after your body dies.

Hebrews 9:27 says, *"And as it is appointed unto men once to die, but after this the judgment."* Simply stated, everybody dies once, and then we stand before God to determine our final eternal destiny.

We'll discuss what God says about "where" in a later chapter, so don't get ahead of me. For now, I want you to simply consider this question.

Would you like to know where you are headed after you die?

If there were a way to know for sure where you would spend eternity, wouldn't you want to know?

This is the trouble with the DO religions. They leave you *wondering* rather than *knowing*. They trap you in a system of insecurity and worry. They leave you thinking "Have I done enough?" "Have I done the right stuff?" "Have I done it right?" Ultimately, you're left wondering "Where am I really headed?"

Once I was speaking about these things with a lady in our community. She was a good lady with a respectable lifestyle, a happy home, and a religious past. Yet, when I asked her if she was sure she was headed to Heaven, her best answer was "I hope so!" Then she got

Chapter Three—Knowing Where You're Going

a puzzled look on her face and simply said, "Can you know that for sure?"

Perhaps you're wondering that now. Can you know for sure?

Friend, the good news is we don't have to speculate about this question. In fact, God doesn't *want* you to speculate or fear your eternity. He does indeed desire for you to know for sure where you are headed! He has gone to great lengths to give you the opportunity to know *for sure* that your eternal destiny is settled.

I want to show you a verse you've probably never seen. Most religious systems tend to avoid this one. It's found in 1 John 5:13, *"These things have I written unto you that believe on the name of the Son of God; that ye may know that ye have eternal life."* Did you catch that? God says, "You may *know* that you have eternal life!"

Think about that for a moment. Let it sink in. Tease it out a bit. God wants you to *know* (that's for sure) where you're going. He doesn't want you to wonder, fear, doubt, or regret. He wants you to know. That's a pretty important verse.

Now think about this question.

Do you know where you are going?

You may hope. You may be thinking optimistically. You may have a good idea of where you are going, but do you KNOW?

The word KNOW implies full confidence and understanding. It removes doubt, hesitation, or question. It *rests* on *fact* rather than *wrestling* with *doubt*. It trusts the truth rather than being frustrated in fear.

What are the implications of "knowing where you're going"? How would this knowledge change your life?

Well, first, it would completely remove the fear of death! This is perhaps the greatest single fear in all the world, and this knowledge could completely remove all doubts. No fear. Just as God says in 2 Timothy 1:7, *"For God hath not given us the spirit of fear; but of power, and of love, and of a sound mind."* God's plans for you do not include fear, but rather a sound mind and a spirit of power and love.

Second, it would give your entire life a different perspective. You would be living *towards* something —preparing for something bigger than life and looking forward to something beyond death. In short, you would have hope!

Chapter Three—Knowing Where You're Going

Friend, you are going somewhere. And God doesn't want you to wonder where. He wants you to settle this matter. He wants you to rest in what you *know*. He wants you to be sure of what will happen to you after you die.

He wants you to *know* that you have eternal life.

Maybe you never saw that verse. Maybe no one ever told you that there's a way to be freed from the fear and doubt that plague so many people when it comes to the subject of death. I hope this is such good news that you will continue reading. The story gets even better.

But let me forewarn you, there's some bad news we must venture into before we get to the best news, so hang in there!

CHAPTER FOUR

Birth Defect

"Do you think I'm a bad person?" Julie asked with great hesitation—almost as if she didn't really want to hear the answer.

I was a college student working a restaurant job, and she was a coworker who had been harshly critical of my faith, even to the point of ridicule.

A few nights prior to this, during closing, she had come into the restaurant stone drunk. After the customers had cleared out, she began to rant and rave against my faith—literally cursing God and telling me how stupid I was for believing in Him.

On this night just a few days later, in the middle of clean up, she stopped me cold in my tracks while I was pushing a vacuum to ask me if I thought she was a bad person.

To be frank, everything in me wanted to say, "Do you think you can curse my God, ridicule my faith, and have me NOT think you're a bad person?" But that would have been judgmental, arrogant, and even hypocritical. It would have been a self-defense mechanism, but not what she most needed to hear.

Deep in their hearts, most people want to believe they are good—even good enough to earn a favorable eternity. On top of that, when you try to tell someone about a failure, the typical response (for any of us) is to defend ourselves. We genuinely want to believe that we are pretty good.

Yet, I've never met someone who would go so far as to say they are perfect. Interesting, isn't it? We wouldn't say that we are perfect, but we don't want to be called bad either. Somehow as humans, we've created this arbitrary gray area that you might call "not too bad."

This gray area soothes the conscience of just about everybody because we each get to draw our own lines and standards, and there's always somebody "worse

Chapter Four—Birth Defect

than us" to whom we compare ourselves. Generally, we reason that we are "pretty good" so long as we can point to someone who is worse than we are! It's like a strange little game we play to try to make ourselves believe we're okay with God.

At that moment at the restaurant, Julie wanted me to say, "Hey, Julie, I know you have your faults, but no, you're not *bad*." After all, with all my faults who am I to criticize her, right?

I could tell that her question was more than a surface concern. She genuinely wanted to know in her heart where I believed she stood with God.

Do you want to know what I told her? I told her what God says.

"Julie, it's not just you…everybody is bad. I'm bad too."

Now, before you get angry and throw this book in the trash, just go with me for a minute.

Her first response was "C'mon, don't preach to me, I want to know what you really think."

In all sincerity, I said, "Julie, we're all bad. I'm bad, you're bad—nobody's perfect!"

Friend, you may not consider yourself "too bad" or "really bad," but you know as well as I do that you're not perfect either.

But where does that leave us? How does God view this imperfection, and where does it place us in His sight? What are the implications of our "imperfections" in light of eternity and where we live after death?

These are weighty questions, but God's word answers them all very clearly. The message isn't so much hidden as ignored or rewritten to fit the religious traditions and agendas of men. When you take God's word at face value, the way He intended it to be taken, it all adds up.

So what does God say? Are we really "all bad"? You may already be defending yourself in your own mind as you read. Don't forget, good news is still ahead, so be willing to let down your self-defense mechanism and listen to God with an open heart. Here's what He says about you and me—and the rest of humanity for that matter.

In Romans 3:23 He says, *"For all have sinned, and come short of the glory of God";* and back just a few verses He says, *"There is none righteous, no, not one"* (Romans 3:10). Simply put, no one is perfect. We all fall short of God's glory or God's perfect standard.

While we might be able to argue that we're better than someone else, we all fall so far short

Chapter Four—Birth Defect

of God's perfection that our petty comparisons become irrelevant.

Think of it this way. What if God commanded us to jump to the moon? You might be able to jump higher than I can, and I might be able to jump higher than my five-year-old grandson can, but in the end, we all fall way short of the goal.

That's what God is saying when He says that we all "fall short of the glory of God." We all fall so far short that the slight difference between your goodness and someone else's goodness (or badness) doesn't matter in God's sight.

Simply put, God says to humanity, "You have a problem. You sin. You are imperfect. You fall short of my glory. You are sinful."

In the next chapter, we'll discover why this is such a problem, but first, we must be willing to admit that the problem exists. For some people, this is a big hurdle.

"I'm just not a bad person," we reason. Compared to someone else, we may not be that bad, but God isn't comparing us to someone else. God's standard is higher than ours. He's using His own perfection—His own holiness and glory are the standard. No matter how good we believe we are, when compared to God's standard, we're all pretty bad.

If the standard is a ten-foot basketball rim, and you can jump high enough to touch it, then you're a good jumper. But if the standard is the moon, and you can only jump to ten feet, then you're not much of a jumper at all.

You might ask, "Well, who could jump to the moon? That's impossible!"

Exactly! It's impossible.

I can imagine you're thinking, "Are you saying that God holds us to an impossible standard?"

Yes, that's what He does according to His own word. He holds us to a perfect standard. Why would He hold us to a perfect standard when He knows that it is impossible for us to meet that standard?

There's only one conclusion. To help us realize that it's not about DO, it's about DONE. It's not about jumping high enough. It's about admitting that we've fallen too far to even *think* of jumping high enough, and then trusting in someone more powerful than ourselves to lift us high enough!

The purpose of God's laws in Scripture is not to *convince* us we can keep them in our own strength or moral efforts, but rather to show us how far we have *fallen from* Him. His requirements are not a mountain we climb to achieve salvation, they are a brick wall we

Chapter Four—Birth Defect

run into that stops us in our tracks, realizing we are hopelessly fallen far from God's original design.

Let's imagine that God literally required us to jump to the moon to get into Heaven. Would you try? Would you despair, or would you ask for a miracle?

One thing is for sure, you would immediately conclude that you couldn't get there on your own.

Friend, that's the point of God's word when He says, *"For there is not a just man upon earth, that doeth good, and sinneth not"* (Ecclesiastes 7:20). He says that our sin and imperfections make even our good works pointless in His sight because our sins literally take us away from Him. *"But we are all as an unclean thing, and all our righteousnesses are as filthy rags; and we all do fade as a leaf; and our iniquities, like the wind, have taken us away"* (Isaiah 64:6).

God wants us to accept the conclusion that we can't get to Him on our own.

God is saying, there is a great distance between us—a distance created by our imperfections. And as we've already concluded, *doing* good things doesn't close the gap. Doing good stuff doesn't pay for bad stuff anymore than not using my Visa card would pay for previous credit debt. Being a good person doesn't negate the bad or in any way undo the sin that we've committed.

God is saying to humanity, "When it comes to your relationship with me, we're divided. You're in way over your head in sinfulness, and you were born that way."

He tells us that we were literally born defective in Psalm 51:5, *"Behold, I was shapen in iniquity; and in sin did my mother conceive me."* In other words, from the moment you were conceived, there was sinfulness in your spiritual genetics. This isn't simply a performance problem or a behavior problem. It's not a *doing* problem, it's a *being* problem.

I am blessed to have three children. You might find this hard to believe, but I didn't deliberately teach any of them to sin. Yet, before they could even talk or walk, they could be selfish. Shortly thereafter they could disobey, display a bad attitude, and throw a temper tantrum. Just a few years into their lives they could lie, fight, argue, and even hurt others. If we didn't teach them to sin, where did all of it come from?

The answer is found in Romans 5:12, *"Wherefore, as by one man sin entered into the world, and death by sin; and so death passed upon all men, for that all have sinned."*

Chapter Four—Birth Defect

Simply put, sin is *in* them, just as it is in every man and woman on the planet. It's *in* us. It's in our spiritual bloodline. From the cradle, every one of us has the natural tendency to do wrong. But you must understand, it's more than just "doing wrong." If it were a behavioral problem, then it would be corrected by good behavior. But God clearly says good behavior cannot correct this problem. It's a state of being. Sin is in us, like a deadly disease. It's literally our spiritual birth defect since Adam and Eve, the first man and woman, chose to sin.

Yes, friend, like it or not, you were born spiritually defective. You were born with a massive spiritual birth defect that makes you imperfect before God and divides you against Him. He says it this way in Ephesians 2:1, *"And you hath he quickened, who were dead in trespasses and sins."*

We'll get back to that verse later, but catch that last part—we were dead in our trespasses and sins. You and I are naturally dead to God spiritually speaking. We are separated from Him because of our sinfulness.

I know this isn't what pop psychology tells you about yourself. It isn't what you want to hear, but do you deny that you are imperfect? Can you accept the fact that you fall short and that your spiritual birth defect has caused a massive separation between you and your Creator?

This sounds like pretty bad news, but sometimes you have to accept bad news before you can apply the good news.

What if you had a treatable form of cancer? Would you want to know the bad news so that your doctor could then give you the good news? Wouldn't you want to hear, "You've got cancer…BUT…we have the cure!"?

Well, before you can understand God's cure, you must accept the diagnosis. God's diagnosis is simple: "You were born spiritually defective, and you are incapable of keeping my perfect standard. Something supernatural must be done to bring you back to me."

Why is this birth defect such a massive problem? Why can't God just wink at our imperfections and move on? Why can't I just say "please forgive me" and life goes on?

These are great questions—let's find out His answers.

CHAPTER FIVE

God's Only Accepted Method of Payment

I have a Visa card that I use for Christmas shopping, family vacations, or on rare occasions for something I want or need.

Imagine if I threw caution to the wind and recklessly charged $10,000 worth of purchases on that card. A month later the statement arrives in my mailbox describing my charges and explaining my payment options.

Rather than pay the debt, let's imagine that I call customer service and explain that I didn't mean to make these charges, that I'm very sorry for making them, and that I will try to do better in the future. Will

Done

that pay my debt? Of course not. (Wouldn't that be nice though?)

Alright, let's try another angle. What if I call customer service and beg and plead for them to forgive my debt? That should take care of it, right? I don't think so.

Well, these Visa card people sure are narrow-minded and legalistic, aren't they? Surely they should be more merciful and forgiving. Surely they aren't being fair!

Friend, my thinking is obviously flawed, even if it is naively sincere. It's not that the Visa card people aren't merciful or patient or kind—it's that they are just and right to expect fair payment for my charges. The issue is not sincerity. The issue is justice. What is right, and who has the authority to say what is right?

I've spoken with many people who say to me, "Well, I ask God to forgive my sin every night before I go to bed." Others have said, "I confess my sin regularly to a priest or to God." Still others have said, "I pay for my sin by doing good."

Friend, God doesn't arbitrarily forgive sin or erase sin's consequences any more than my credit card bank would arbitrarily erase my debt simply because I asked.

Chapter Five—God's Only Accepted Method of Payment

No, the credit card bank has determined a *method of payment*. Apart from that method of payment, nothing else will erase my debt on that card. This is not unfair or unjust. Quite the contrary, it's reasonable. It's just and right. I can't send them an apology note, a Thanksgiving food basket, or even a Walmart gift card. I must send them one form of payment—money. This is the established standard and practice of credit card companies. I don't argue it, I just accept and respond to their set standard.

In much the same way, God as the just judge and ruler of the universe is holy—perfect, right, and pure in every way. As such, His purity requires only one acceptable payment for sin or evil. Yes, sin must be paid for. Why? Because God is just and good. A good God would never permit something as horrible as sin and death to run rampant in time and eternity forever. No, a good and all-powerful God would deal with sin once and for all—like a just judge—so that we could ultimately be freed from it for all of eternity. You see, God's goodness requires that He take action against something so destructive as sin.

This is one reason He describes Himself as a just judge that will bring judgment. If there is no ultimate judge, what hope would there be for the world? But if there is, what hope is there for me and you?

Long before you and I were born—long before the world was created, God determined that sin, evil, and death would have to die. This is not negotiable. It is just and fair and, yes, it is even good considering the terrible power and destruction that comes with sin and death.

Think about it. Every undesirable aspect of human life on earth is a product of sin and our fallen condition of rebellion against our Creator—from crime to political oppression to wars to hurricanes to death itself. So, yes, all the injustice and suffering of human history deserves ultimate judgment, and any reasonable heart secretly hopes that there is a good judge who will ultimately bring an end to suffering and sin.

What is the only acceptable payment for sin?

God says in Romans 6:23, *"For the wages of sin is death."* Death. Seems like a high payment, right? Sounds pretty bad? Well, let's take a second look.

Why would a *good* God let sin *live*? That would be infinitely worse than our United States justice system allowing murder and mayhem. If our justice system accepted such atrocities, it would no longer be a "good

Chapter Five—God's Only Accepted Method of Payment

system." Even so, if God were to allow sin and evil to continue for eternity, He wouldn't be a good God.

No, His goodness requires that He take action. His justice requires payment, and long before you or I came along, God determined that there was only one final outcome for sin—there was only one acceptable solution for something so deadly and destructive. Death.

Sin must die. Death must die. These things that are so evil and destructive must face the only just end—the only acceptable outcome—they must be locked away in a final prison. Sin is *so* bad that God has determined once and for all—sin must die.

Do you recognize God's goodness and love as displayed through this death sentence? He refuses to allow that which is harmful to plague us forever. He loves us too much. His goodness is too good. He cannot allow sin to go on destroying the world.

Imagine that there was a murderer living on your block. This murderer kills at will and has no preference for his victims. He kills men, women, and children with no warning and no remorse.

Imagine that you know who he is, and you've called the police only to find out they already know who the killer is. Imagine that they've decided to let him continue killing. No penalty. No prosecution. No justice. Imagine that the police investigators tell you, "We've decided just to be good on this one. A loving police department would never send anyone to prison."

You would be outraged! You would do whatever it took to make sure this man received justice and to restore peace and safety in your community!

Have you ever heard someone say, "Well I just can't believe a *loving* God would create Hell" or "I don't believe a loving God would ever judge sin"? Friend, how could a loving God *not* do something about all the terrible things that exist in life? How could a loving God allow sin to go free and not act?

He can't. He won't.

God's word teaches very clearly that when time comes to an end, God will bring a final judgment on sin and death. He will demand final payment, and He only accepts one form of payment for sin—death.

In fact, God has created a final prison for sin and death—a final resting place. It's called "the lake of fire." Revelation 20:14 speaks of this final judgment, *"And death and hell were cast into the lake of fire. This is the second death."*

Chapter Five—God's Only Accepted Method of Payment

Friend, this is not mean, unjust, or unfair. It's a *good* thing that God will send sin and death to an eternal resting place!

Here's where it gets hard to accept. Let me remind you again, we're not looking for "man's opinion" here. We're seeking God's stated truth. We're trying to understand His terms of justice.

God's word is clear in Matthew 25:41 that God didn't originally create Hell for men and women. It was intended for the devil and his angels. *"Then shall he say also unto them on the left hand, Depart from me, ye cursed, into everlasting fire, prepared for the devil and his angels."* God's original intent after passing final judgment on the devil and sin was to bring men and women into an eternal, loving relationship with Him. His plan is born out of a loving heart and a good nature. He is perfect—perfectly loving, perfectly good, but also perfectly just.

Because God's justice system demands payment for sin—death, and because I was born defective with sin flowing in my spiritual blood veins, I now have a very serious predicament.

As a sinner, I have a sin debt that must be paid. There is a minimum wage for my sin—a law in God's justice that demands payment. Sin now stands between me and God. While God *loves me*, He *hates sin*. If He didn't *hate sin*, He couldn't *love me*. It's like saying if your loved one has cancer that you can't love your relative and love the cancer at the same time. If you love your relative, you will hate the cancer and desire to remove it if possible. If you loved the cancer, you would make yourself an enemy to your relative.

This is exactly what the Bible means when it says *"the carnal mind is enmity against God"* (Romans 8:7). Whether or not you feel warm and fuzzy about God, though He loves you very much, your sin makes you His enemy.

Ouch! That hurts. Maybe that's a tough pill to swallow, but it is exactly God's diagnosis and message to us.

No wonder I can't earn my way or do good things to gain God's approval. Sin stands in the way, like a giant canyon, dividing me from all that God intended.

In short, my sin condemns me in the sight of God.

Don't get me wrong. This doesn't mean that God doesn't love me. We'll get to that in a moment. It simply means that if something miraculous doesn't happen—if God doesn't find a way to intervene—I'm doomed.

Chapter Five—God's Only Accepted Method of Payment

Though God loves me, He cannot allow sin into Heaven. He cannot allow sin to live, and since I have sin in me, I'm marked for death. He doesn't want me to spend one second apart from Him in Hell—this was never His intention. But that's what will happen if a miracle doesn't occur.

My sin must be paid for. That's God's law. My sin must die. That's God's goodness. It's like saying "cancer must be cured!" What is the cure? Well, we know it isn't being good. No matter how good or religious I am, I still have sin in me. Remember, it's not a *behavior* problem, it's a *being* problem. Being good doesn't pay for sin.

Only one thing pays for sin. Death. Death is the only viable option for something so horrific.

If I stand before God with sin recorded against my name—if I face Him as a sinner, there's only one final destination for me according to His own words:

> *And the sea gave up the dead which were in it; and death and hell delivered up the dead which were in them: and they were judged every man according to their works. And death and hell were cast into the lake of fire. This is the second death.*—Revelation 20:13-14

Done

> *But the fearful, and unbelieving, and the abominable, and murderers, and whoremongers, and sorcerers, and idolaters, and all liars, shall have their part in the lake which burneth with fire and brimstone: which is the second death.*
> —Revelation 21:8

Yes, this lake of fire (according to God) is a real place, a terrible place, and men do end up there because of their sins. It's not God's desire; it's not what He wants for you, but it is the final resting place of sin. Apart from a miracle, all who sin are headed there because God is too good to let sin live.

Twice in these verses God refers to a second death. In other words, we all die once, then we stand before God where it is determined whether we live on forever with God, or whether we die a second time. The second death is eternal separation from God in the lake of fire. It is final—unchangeable. It is not where God wants us to spend eternity, but it is the only just and reasonable payment for sin.

God calls it "being condemned" in Romans 5:18, *"Therefore as by the offence of one judgment came upon all men to condemnation."*

Friend, because of our sin, we stand condemned before God. We are all guilty. *"Therefore thou art*

Chapter Five—God's Only Accepted Method of Payment

inexcusable" (Romans 2:1). We are without excuse. Our sin debt must be paid. No ifs, ands, or buts. Sin must die.

Because God is good, because God is just, because God is love—He must put to death every bad thing. Yet, because God loves me, He doesn't want me to face this curse. Since I'm born into sin, I'm a condemned man, no matter how good I've been.

Pretty terrible predicament we're in, isn't it?

Yes, there is a minimum wage law. Yes, there is a second death. Yes to these things because God is good and just—because He is perfectly pure and cannot simply ignore evil.

And yes, unless God miraculously intervenes, you and I will face that second death.

We've fallen too far to jump to the moon. We have failed God's perfect standard. Saving ourselves is impossible. We have accrued a debt that we cannot pay, and there's only one form of payment accepted.

But there is a very important three-letter word that makes all the difference: BUT.

"For the wages of sin is death, BUT…" (Romans 6:23).

A miracle did happen.

CHAPTER SIX

Can I Get a Substitute?

Imagine what the response of the Visa card bank would be if I continually called customer service asking them to forgive my debt or if I kept sending them food baskets and care packages as payment. I think the end message would be something along the lines of, "Forget it, pay your debt, and if you can't, then find someone who can!"

Think about that. Find someone who *can*. Now there's an idea. Find someone who can either give or loan me the money to pay my debt. After all, they don't care who pays the debt, they just want the debt paid, but it must be paid on *their terms*, not mine.

Sadly, the world is filled with very sincere people who are trying to pay their sin debt their *own way* rather than God's. It's not a new scheme. In fact, the first person to do this was named Cain.

In Genesis, the first book of the Bible, Cain brought God an offering—a payment for his sins—but he did it *his* way. He refused to bring the payment that God required, and so his offering was refused (Genesis 4:1–7). God was basically saying, "Sin must be paid for on my terms, not yours."

Strangely, Cain got very angry with God for rejecting his offering, but it was his own choice—his own pride got in the way. Perhaps as you've been reading, you're tempted to respond to this message in self-justification or self-defense. Perhaps you're offended to find out that your goodness doesn't hold water with God. I hope you will let down your pride and not allow it to stand between you and the miracle that God provided.

Pride would be a silly reason to let sin win!

Unfortunately, there will be many people at the final judgment of sin who did many good things "for God," but they will still have an unpaid sin debt. Their DOING for God won't be enough.

Chapter Six—Can I Get a Substitute?

In Matthew 7:21–23, Jesus brings a stern warning to those who try to take care of their sin debt their own way: *"Not every one that saith unto me, Lord, Lord, shall enter into the kingdom of heaven; but he that doeth the will of my Father which is in heaven."* In other words, entrance into Heaven is gained God's way and only God's way.

He continues, *"Many will say to me in that day, Lord, Lord, have we not prophesied in thy name? and in thy name have cast out devils? and in thy name done many wonderful works? And then will I profess unto them, I never knew you: depart from me, ye that work iniquity."*

Many people will begin rehearsing all the good things they did for God, but the final word will be when God says, "I never knew you." In other words, "You never came to Me *my* way. Your sin debt remains unpaid."

When He says, *"Depart from me,"* that's the second death—eternal separation from God.

What is God's way? We will come to it more fully, but here's a hint. When confronting those who were trying to DO many good works to gain salvation, Jesus said these very simple words, *"This is the work of God, that ye believe on him whom he hath sent"* (John 6:29). Hmmm—a very interesting statement!

Friend, this is a very serious matter. God is good, loving, and merciful; yet, God is also just, holy, and perfect. As a sinful man, I stand before Him loved by His great heart, yet condemned by His great justice.

Before God can accept me, He must first completely remove my sin and justly resolve it. Otherwise, he would be accepting sin rather than judging it as any good judge would do. Once sin is paid, He is then free to welcome me into His family and into an eternal relationship with Him, but the debt must be paid *before* any of this can happen.

Cue the good news! A miracle did happen! You see, God *"is longsuffering to us-ward, not willing that any should perish, but that all should come to repentance"* (2 Peter 3:9). God doesn't desire that a single person face His judgment on sin. He doesn't want you to face eternal separation from Him in Hell.

In the last chapter, we saw this verse, *"For the wages of sin is death...."* The last half of this verse is where the good news truly begins. It says, *"but the gift of God is eternal life through Jesus Christ our Lord"* (Romans 6:23).

Chapter Six—Can I Get a Substitute?

What if I *couldn't* pay my credit card debt, but you *could*? What if you were my friend and you loved me enough to write a check and offer it to me as a free gift? Would this work? Would Visa accept your money on my behalf? Of course!

This is called "substitution." In other words, your money is being substituted for my lack. So long as I accept your gift, it could be applied to my account and my debt could be legally and justly erased.

Substitute. We have lots of substitutes in life. Salt substitutes. Sugar substitutes. Meat substitutes (Ugh!). We have substitute teachers, substitute hair, and even substitute teeth. A substitute is a stand-in—a replacement for the original, and in most cases, substitutes are inferior to the original. In God's plan, this isn't the case. His substitute is far superior!

Understanding that we're guilty before God and condemned by sin, understanding that sin must die and that death is the only acceptable outcome, and understanding that if I pay for my own sin it will require eternal separation from God—there's only one possible solution.

I would ask God this question:
"Can I get a substitute?"

Is there anyone or anything that can pay this debt *for me*? Am I doomed or is there a stand-in?

God's answer quite simply is "Yes, there is a substitute." There is someone who can take your death. There is someone who can be the "go-between" —someone who can pay the debt to satisfy God's justice and give you eternal life all at the same time.

If you are curious about who took your death, then keep reading. Let's find out more about this substitute.

CHAPTER SEVEN

God's Only Miraculous Substitute

First, understand this isn't just *any* substitute. I can't pay for your sins. You can't pay for mine. In fact, no mere human being can pay for the sins of another because we're all under the same debt. We're all made of the same stuff—a sinful nature.

And remember this isn't just a performance or behavior problem, it's a *being* problem. The problem isn't just what I've *done*, it's who I *am* and what is inside of me.

For this reason, this substitute must be an amazing kind of miraculous substitute that not only pays for my sin, but also completely *removes* it from me and *destroys* it forever. This miracle requires a kind of spiritual surgery that removes the cancer of sin and creates in me a new identity, one that isn't sinful before God.

I need a substitute who can change the inside of me from being *sinful* to being *righteous* before God. I need a substitute who will die the death that sin requires once and for all. I need more than a surface makeover—I need a *complete spiritual rebuild.*

Jesus actually called it "rebirth." In John 3, Jesus is approached by a very religious man—a very good man. This was a man who had spent his life *doing* very good things for God, and Jesus says to him in verse 3, *"Verily, verily, I say unto thee, Except a man be born again, he cannot see the kingdom of God."* Unless you have a complete spiritual rebirth, unless we can change your spiritual identity from sinful to righteous, you cannot enter Heaven.

Again He said in John 3:7, *"Marvel not that I said unto thee, Ye must be born again."* When this man was astounded at Jesus' requirement, he asked, *"How can a man be born when he is old?"* Then Jesus said, *"Except a man be born of water and of the Spirit, he cannot enter into the kingdom of God."* Your first birth (by water) was physical, but your second birth (by spirit) must be

Chapter Seven—God's Only Miraculous Substitute

spiritual. This isn't something you can see with your eyes—it's something you experience in your heart.

A substitute. This is a miraculous stand-in—the kind of substitute that doesn't just pay a debt, but the kind that completely rebuilds me and gives me a new spiritual bloodline. This is the kind of substitute that both pays for sin and gives me a whole new identity with God, one without sin and without debt.

So, who is this substitute?

Here's what God says, *"For when we were yet without strength, in due time Christ died for the ungodly"* (Romans 5:6). Again He says, *"But God commendeth his love toward us, in that, while we were yet sinners, Christ died for us"* (Romans 5:8). God sums it up in Romans 5:19 when He says, *"For as by one man's disobedience many were made sinners, so by the obedience of one shall many be made righteous."*

Jesus personally stated, *"I am the good shepherd: the good shepherd giveth his life for the sheep"* (John 10:11).

In John 14:6, Jesus was telling His disciples that He was preparing to go back to Heaven to prepare a place for them. During the conversation, one of His disciples asked, "How do we get there?" Amazingly, this is exactly what Jesus said to him, *"I am the way, the truth, and the life: no man cometh unto the Father, but by me."*

That is an exclusive statement! Jesus said, "If you ever hope to come to God, you must go through me." He didn't say you must go through baptism, through a church, through a priest, or through any other way. He didn't say, "*There* is the way." He said, "*I* am the way." He said, "I am the *only* way." He is the only substitute for our sin. He is the only hope for our souls.

Many religions have mediators or "go-betweens" to bring men to God. Some call them priests or bishops, but the basic intent is that this man helps bring you to God in some way that you cannot come to Him yourself. This is called a "mediator"—a go-between—like a defense attorney advocating for you before a judge.

God identified Jesus clearly when He said, *"For there is one God, and one mediator between God and men, the man Christ Jesus; Who gave himself a ransom for all"* (1 Timothy 2:5–6). In other words, Jesus is the only mediator you ever need!

In Hebrews 2:9, God says, *"But we see Jesus, who was made a little lower than the angels for the suffering of death, crowned with glory and honour; that he by the grace of God should taste death for every man."*

Chapter Seven—God's Only Miraculous Substitute

Yes, God did provide an amazing, miraculous substitute to die our death, to take away our sins, and to rebirth us spiritually so that we could come to Him.

Jesus is our substitute.

Jesus is *your* substitute.

God's answer? Yes, you can have a substitute, but this substitute must be more than just a man. The only solution was for God to take the form of a man, come to Earth, live a sinless life, and personally die for us.

Yes, Jesus is God.

If you think that's an extreme claim, consider this: first of all, He repeatedly said that He was God. Here's one example: *"He that hath seen me hath seen the Father; and how sayest thou then, Shew us the Father?"* (John 14:9). Good men or good teachers don't go around claiming that they are God.

Second, He not only died, but He rose from the dead! All over the world, you can visit the burial places of religious leaders and founders of worldwide religious systems for every religion but one—true Christianity. When you visit Jesus' tomb, it's wide open and empty.

Historical fact very much supports the literal resurrection of Jesus Christ. Consider this. After Jesus died, His followers went back to their old jobs—fishing.

They rejected Him. Their dream was dead. These weren't the kind of guys who would die for a lie, much less take on the most powerful Roman guards to break into a tomb and steal a dead body.

The morning after their return to fishing, something life-changing and miraculous happened that caused them to leave fishing for the rest of their lives. They also died horrible deaths for the message they preached—that Jesus died and rose again.

Let me ask you this question. Would you die for what you knew to be a lie? I doubt it.

The fact that the disciples died for their message, every one of them, is proof enough that Jesus truly rose from the dead. We know Jesus is God because He is the only man who ever conquered death and proved it undeniably. *"But now is Christ risen from the dead"* (1 Corinthians 15:20).

Third, we know Jesus is God because it's the only viable option. There are only three things Jesus could have been—God in the flesh, a liar, or a crazy man. One author put it this way—Lord, liar, or lunatic. He was much too wise and His ministry too powerful to call Him "crazy." He couldn't have been lying because, again, His teaching was too true, and He *and* His followers all would have died for the lie. His miracles,

Chapter Seven—God's Only Miraculous Substitute

His life-changing three-year ministry, and His literal resurrection from death all prove that He was God in the flesh.

If you refuse to believe that Jesus is God, you must throw out the entire Bible because this fact is woven like a thread into every page! Colossians 1:15 calls Him *"the image of the invisible God."* First Timothy 3:16 clearly states, *"And without controversy great is the mystery of godliness: God was manifest in the flesh, justified in the Spirit, seen of angels, preached unto the Gentiles, believed on in the world, received up into glory."*

Jesus personally fulfilled dozens of Bible prophecies where God promised to send us a Savior. These were things completely out of His control, like where and when He would be born, who His parents were, and how He would die. Every single prophecy was fulfilled perfectly just as the Bible predicted. For thousands of years God promised to send this substitute, and when He came, He came just as God said He would.

Yes, Jesus is God in the flesh (John 1:14). He came to Earth for one reason—it was the only way to rescue us from the ruthless enemy of sin. This enemy had so invaded our world that it was holding us hostage to condemnation. God loves us so much that He literally came to Earth to rescue us.

He came to us because we could have never come to Him! Jesus coming says that our fallen and lost condition was so desperate that only desperate measures could save the day. We couldn't save ourselves. God Himself had to intervene. And He did! He is a Divine Hero on a cosmic rescue mission for your soul. You are the precious object of His infinite love.

Do you want to know about the battle He had to fight and the darkness He had to face to rescue you? Of course you do.

The story is about to get even better!

CHAPTER EIGHT

Paid in Full

Perhaps you've seen images or heard descriptions of what Jesus went through on the cross. It was the most gruesome and most tormenting death that the Roman authorities of that time could produce. It was carried out by highly skilled Roman guards who were trained to inflict the most pain over the longest possible time. It was a slow and brutal method of execution and the most publicly humiliating way to die. The pain was so bad that we created a new word to describe it —*excruciating* (Latin: *crux*—cross, crucifixion).

In Jesus' case, He was first beaten with fists and spit on during a series of rigged court trials. During this time His beard was forcefully ripped from His face, and His head was crowned with long thorns. These thorns deeply pierced His head between His skin and skull, creating excruciating pain and bleeding.

After this brutal beating, He was sentenced to being brutally lacerated over and over with an object of torture called the "cat-of-nine-tails." This leather whip had nine leather straps at the end, each embedded with sharp shards of metal, bone, or rock so that the lashing would tear and rip the flesh. The guards trained in using this whip were highly skilled at damaging the human body without bringing death. It was a horrific and bloody method of torture.

Finally, Jesus—barely alive—was forced to carry a large wooden crossbeam through a jeering crowd in Jerusalem to a public place of execution that we call Calvary. In that place, He willingly laid upon that crossbeam and lovingly opened His arms wide.

At that point, the executioners hammered long iron nails into Jesus' hands and feet, painfully affixing Him to the cross. Then he was publicly lifted up and put on display. He suffered and agonized for six hours until He willingly gave up His life.

He did that for you and me.

Let that sink in. Let that change you.

Chapter Eight—Paid in Full

That's how much God loves you.

God told this story long before it happened when He gave us the following prophecy from Isaiah 53. As you read this, realize it is talking about what Jesus did for you personally.

> *He is despised and rejected of men; a man of sorrows, and acquainted with grief: and we hid as it were our faces from him; he was despised, and we esteemed him not. Surely he hath borne our griefs, and carried our sorrows: yet we did esteem him stricken, smitten of God, and afflicted. But he was wounded for our transgressions, he was bruised for our iniquities: the chastisement of our peace was upon him; and with his stripes we are healed.*
>
> *All we like sheep have gone astray; we have turned every one to his own way; and the LORD hath laid on him the iniquity of us all. He was oppressed, and he was afflicted, yet he opened not his mouth: he is brought as a lamb to the slaughter, and as a sheep before her shearers is dumb, so he openeth not his mouth. He was taken from prison and from judgment: and who shall declare his generation? for he was cut off out of the land of the living: for the transgression of my people was he stricken. And he made his*

> *grave with the wicked, and with the rich in his death; because he had done no violence, neither was any deceit in his mouth.*
>
> *Yet it pleased the LORD to bruise him; he hath put him to grief: when thou shalt make his soul an offering for sin, he shall see his seed, he shall prolong his days, and the pleasure of the LORD shall prosper in his hand.* —Isaiah 53:3–10

Would you take a moment now and reread that portion of the Bible? Ask God to help you truly understand His message to you. It tells the story of exactly what Jesus was doing when He gave His life on that cross. He was giving His life for our transgressions (our sin) and making Himself the offering (the payment).

While on the cross, Jesus made several statements. Perhaps the most important one was this, *"It is finished"* (John 19:30).

Done.

What was He saying? What does "It is finished" mean?

Literally, it means "paid in full." It means the complete and final payment for every sin you ever commit is now paid. This includes all your sins —past, present, and future—even the ones you haven't committed yet.

Chapter Eight—Paid in Full

His sacrifice was that comprehensive.

Jesus was God's miraculous intervention. He was God on a divine rescue mission to save humanity from the power of sin and the condemnation that it brings. Jesus was the miracle!

After He died, a Roman soldier pierced His side with a spear—verifying His death and yet again fulfilling a specific ancient prophecy (Psalm 34:20), proving that He was who He said.

He was buried in a borrowed tomb, and after three days He literally conquered death and rose to life again! He was seen by hundreds of people for over forty days. The Bible says in Acts 1:3, *"To whom also he shewed himself alive after his passion by many infallible proofs, being seen of them forty days, and speaking of the things pertaining to the kingdom of God."*

Did you see that? Infallible proof! Jesus' resurrection isn't just a myth, a legend, or a lie—it was proven infallibly.

What does this mean for you?

First, Jesus' death paid the price for your sin. Your debt can truly be paid and forgiven because of what He accomplished when He said "It is finished!" Paid in full!

Done.

Second, His resurrection made a new birth possible. Remember the "complete spiritual rebuild" that we talked about? Because Jesus conquered death completely, He not only offers you payment for sins, He offers you a brand new kind of life—a brand new spiritual identity. The miracle can be complete because He rose again! You can have a complete re-engineering of your spiritual genetic system, your identity with God, which makes you a new creature in His sight. You no longer have to remain a sinful creature but a new creature with no sin debt.

This is what DONE is all about. This is what "It is finished" means.

The Bible uses a great word to describe this "paid in full" concept. The word is *propitiation*, and it simply means "the full payment for." Here's where it is used:

> *Whom God hath set forth to be a propitiation through faith in his blood, to declare his righteousness for the remission of sins that are past, through the forbearance of God.*
> —Romans 3:25

> *And he is the propitiation for our sins: and not for ours only, but also for the sins of the whole world.*
> —1 John 2:2

Chapter Eight—Paid in Full

> *Herein is love, not that we loved God, but that he loved us, and sent his Son to be the propitiation for our sins.* —1 John 4:10

The Bible also calls what Jesus did "reconciliation." Just as you reconcile a relationship when it experiences a division, Jesus brought reconciliation between us and God. He says in 2 Corinthians 5:18–19, *"And all things are of God, who hath reconciled us to himself by Jesus Christ, and hath given to us the ministry of reconciliation; To wit, that God was in Christ, reconciling the world unto himself, not imputing their trespasses unto them; and hath committed unto us the word of reconciliation."*

In verse 21 He says again, *"For he hath made him to be sin for us, who knew no sin; that we might be made the righteousness of God in him."* God made Jesus "sin" so that we could be made "righteous." Amazing! What an incredible gift! What indescribable love!

The Bible is filled with similar verses which explain in detail that Jesus Christ was our substitute and that He paid our debt in full. Take a moment and ask God to help you understand His message in these verses.

> *Who gave himself for our sins, that he might deliver us from this present evil world,*

according to the will of God and our Father.
—Galatians 1:4

Who his own self bare our sins in his own body on the tree, that we, being dead to sins, should live unto righteousness: by whose stripes ye were healed.—1 Peter 2:24

For Christ also hath once suffered for sins, the just for the unjust, that he might bring us to God, being put to death in the flesh, but quickened by the Spirit.—1 Peter 3:18

But if we walk in the light, as he is in the light, we have fellowship one with another, and the blood of Jesus Christ his Son cleanseth us from all sin.
—1 John 1:7

And from Jesus Christ, who is the faithful witness, and the first begotten of the dead, and the prince of the kings of the earth. Unto him that loved us, and washed us from our sins in his own blood.
—Revelation 1:5

Let me conclude this chapter with one final thought. Jesus' payment for your sin was not *partial*—it was a *full* payment.

Chapter Eight—Paid in Full

I once shared this with a man who seemed to struggle with understanding the concept of a "full payment." After what seemed like hours of trying to get through to him, it was like the light bulb came on in his head.

He smiled and said, "All my life I've understood that Jesus paid for my sins, but I've believed that it was a two-way deal—like a 50/50 proposition. In other words, Jesus did His part but I still must do my part. But if I understand what you're saying, then Jesus did it *all*, and I can't do anything. It's 100% Jesus and 0% me!"

Exactly. This is not a 50/50 proposition. Jesus didn't pay for part of your sin and then give you the rest of the bill to pay. He didn't say "It is almost finished." He didn't say "It is partially paid." He said, "It is fully paid."

Even religions that claim to believe in Jesus seem to teach that He only paid for *part* of our sins. Many teach that there is still much that you must DO to make atonement for your sin—as though Jesus made partial payment and you must make the rest. This simply isn't the message of the Bible.

Jesus paid it all! DONE.

Are you understanding this? You don't have to pay for your own sin. A miracle of divine intervention happened! God stepped in and took your punishment—*all of it*!

Now the question is this. How does this wonderful payment for my sin actually get *applied* to my account? How can Jesus' death be applied to me?

Well, one thing we've concluded for sure—it won't involve DOING! But it will involve *deciding*.

Would you believe it's a gift?

How much better can this get?!

CHAPTER NINE

The Greatest Gift

Christmas around our house is a greatly anticipated event! Probably much like you, we save and plan for months. Way ahead of time, the kids (and now grandkids) take inventory of what they don't have —stuff they can ask for on their Christmas lists. I mean we're getting hints somewhere around August. Wow, do they get creative and does the list ever grow over those few months before Christmas!

I remember one year my son wanted a guitar, a bunk bed, a bike, and a new music player. That's the shortlist, and at the time, there were still eight weeks until Christmas!

Done

No doubt, as the time draws nearer, my wife and I will carve out some time and venture into that jungle we call the mall to do some Christmas shopping with the rest of the crowd. At that time, we will take our hard-earned cash and spend it to provide gifts for our whole family—the grown kids, their spouses, and all the grandkids.

Catch this. No one *makes* us do this—we pay the full price for the gifts because we love our family. It's our delight to love them.

Then on Christmas morning (or sooner if we get talked into it), these gifts are freely presented to all our "crazed" grandkids who couldn't wait for this moment to arrive!

No doubt you even enjoy getting a gift or two yourself each Christmas or birthday. There's something nice about receiving a gift.

One thing about Christmas—though we talk for months about the kids "being good" or they won't get anything for Christmas, they all know that's a joke. In truth, they know they're going to get gifts no matter how good or bad they've been, and usually it's plenty of both!

Even a child understands that a gift isn't about DOING, it's about DONE. In other words, no ten-

Chapter Nine—The Greatest Gift

year-old expects to have to pay for Christmas gifts. It's generally understood among the preschool, elementary, teenage, and even young adult population of the world that Christmas gifts are paid for by parents and received by kids! It's like a global law.

Well friend, when God refers to the payment for your sins—salvation from Hell—He calls it a gift. It's a gift *from* Him *to* you provided *through* Jesus Christ. And it is *His delight* to love you and offer you this gift which He purchased at so high a price.

Romans 6:23 says, *"For the wages of sin is death; but the gift of God is eternal life through Jesus Christ our Lord."* Plain and simple—it's a gift of God.

John 3:16 begins, *"For God so loved the world, that he **gave** his only begotten Son...."*

Many times in Scripture God tells us that salvation is a gift. Look at these verses carefully and see how many times God refers to this gift:

> *But not as the offence, so also is the free gift. For if through the offence of one many be dead, much more the grace of God, and the gift by grace, which is by one man, Jesus Christ, hath abounded unto many. And not as it was by one that sinned, so is the gift: for the judgment was*

> *by one to condemnation, but the free gift is of many offences unto justification. For if by one man's offence death reigned by one; much more they which receive abundance of grace and of the gift of righteousness shall reign in life by one, Jesus Christ.) Therefore as by the offence of one judgment came upon all men to condemnation; even so by the righteousness of one the free gift came upon all men unto justification of life.*
> —Romans 5:15–18

The central message here is that as sin came upon all men because of Adam's sin, even so God's free gift of salvation (justification and righteousness) is made available to all men through one person—Jesus.

The word *justification* means "to declare righteous." The word *righteous* means "perfect or right in God's sight." This is the message: For God to declare me righteous (not guilty), it must come through the gift of Jesus Christ.

Again in 2 Corinthians 9:15 we read, *"Thanks be unto God for his unspeakable gift."* And finally in Ephesians 2:8 God says, *"For by grace are ye saved through faith; and that not of yourselves: it is the gift of God."*

Chapter Nine—The Greatest Gift

Without a doubt, this is the greatest gift that you've ever been offered. It beats every Christmas and every birthday of your entire life all put together! This gift determines your eternity with God in Heaven.

There are two things you must realize about a gift.

First, it must be *completely free* or it's not a gift. Even my computer knows this. Every time I write "free gift," my autocorrect tries to tell me to delete the word "free" because there is no other kind of gift.

A true gift cannot be paid for or earned. A true gift has no conditions or strings attached. It must be paid for by another and then offered freely. If you must earn, deserve, pay, or in any way compensate for a gift, it is no longer a gift.

That's what God means in this verse, *"And if by grace, then is it no more of works: otherwise grace is no more grace. But if it be of works, then is it no more grace: otherwise work is no more work"* (Romans 11:6).

Grace is *getting* what I *don't* deserve. Mercy is *not* getting what I *do* deserve. *Mercy* is when the police officer pulls you over for speeding but lets you off with a warning. *Grace* would be the same police officer pulling you over for speeding and giving you a $100 Walmart gift card just because he loves you!

With this gift from God, you are being offered both God's *grace* and God's *mercy*. In mercy, He is withholding what we actually deserve (judgment), and in grace He is offering what we could never deserve (eternal life and love).

In many ways, God calls this a gift of His grace—something given from unmerited favor. Titus 2:11 says, *"For the grace of God that bringeth salvation hath appeared to all men."*

Hebrews 2:9 says, *"But we see Jesus, who was made a little lower than the angels for the suffering of death, crowned with glory and honour; that he by the grace of God should taste death for every man."*

The second thing about a gift is that it must be *optional*. A forced gift is no gift at all. A gift cannot be forced upon the recipient—it can only be offered.

Are you seeing God's message? God's truth to us isn't DO—it's DONE! In so many ways He tries to tell us that eternal life is a gift that has been purchased by the death of Jesus Christ. It cannot be earned, paid for, or deserved. It's already paid in full.

The full pardon for your sins is gift-wrapped and waiting under the tree upon which Jesus died for you. It was paid for by the precious life and blood of Jesus Christ who died in your place. He offers this gift to you

Chapter Nine—The Greatest Gift

freely, by His love and grace. It cost Him His life, and He is eager for you to accept it as your own.

He will not force you to take it, and He cannot accept your efforts to earn it. Yet, He longs for you to have it!

Remember 2 Peter 3:9 says that God *"is longsuffering to us-ward, not willing that any should perish, but that all should come to repentance."* God will not force you to come to repentance—for you to recognize your sin debt and come to Him for the only cure. He will never force Himself on you. He's not that kind of God.

He has DONE everything necessary, including putting this little book into your hands. He has paid the price in full for this gift, and now He presents you with a decision…

If you'd like to know how to make this gift your own, then let's keep talking.

CHAPTER TEN

Believing on Christ

What if Christmas morning came and my kids and grandkids refused to open their gifts? (Probably won't happen, but go with me on this one for a moment!) That would be a terrible disappointment. After all the trouble of purchasing, wrapping, and waiting in eager anticipation, we would be terribly let down if the kids didn't want what we had purchased for them.

Now, in all reality, that's highly unlikely! Why? Because receiving a gift is easy. It's fun. It's something you look forward to and anticipate. I've never once had to coax my family members to open a gift. I've never had to talk them into it. I've never had to wait while they decided whether to take it or not. I've never had to convince them that my gift was good.

No, they seem to cross those bridges quickly. In no time flat, as soon as we allow them, they are tearing wrapping paper from everything in sight.

So why do so many people hesitate to receive a gift from the Heavenly Father?

I've shared this news with so many people who can't seem to decide what to do with it. They hesitate. They struggle with belief. They can't seem to accept that God made it this simple. They reason that there must be more to it!

God couldn't let me off the hook that easily, they think. *There must be a catch. There must be something I have to do to earn it or pay for it.*

No matter how you look at it, if you choose to believe God's word, then you have to go with DONE, not DO.

And if you go with DONE, if you accept that salvation (the payment for sin) is a free gift, then there are only two simple decisions remaining to actually make this gift yours.

You see, to receive any gift you must make two simple decisions—the first is internal and the

Chapter Ten—Believing on Christ

second is external. This happens almost naturally and subconsciously with most gifts.

It goes like this.

If I walked up to you on the street and offered you $1,000 in cash as a free gift, you would have two quick decisions.

***Decision #1**—Do I believe this guy?*

You would stand there a moment, look at me, check me out, and try to assess what I'm up to. You would try to quickly evaluate whether you believe or disbelieve my offer. In all likelihood you would be suspicious—maybe so much so that you would choose *not* to believe and would go on your merry way. In this case, the second decision becomes irrelevant.

Yet, if you choose to believe me, your internal choice is complete and your external choice is this:

***Decision #2**—Will I receive this gift?*

Even though you believe that I'm offering you $1,000, you could still opt not to take the gift. You could say, "Thanks, but no thanks." You could say, "Looks like you need it more than I do, pal!" You could choose to walk away. Though you believe, you could still choose to reject the gift.

You see, on the side of the giver, a true gift must be *free* and *optional*, and on the side of the receiver, a true gift must be *believed* and *received*!

For a gift to become yours, you must choose to believe the giver and to receive it as your own. Until you make these two simple decisions, the gift is not truly yours. It could be paid for. It could be wrapped and waiting. It could have your name on it. But if you don't believe it and receive it, then it will never be yours.

So it is with the gift of God—eternal life. You don't get this gift by default. You get this gift by decision. Yes, it's paid for. Yes, it's ready and waiting for you. Yes, it has your name on it. And yes, you could decide to walk away. You could decide you don't believe and you won't receive. It would be the worst decision you could ever make.

Now we understand why Jesus said those words, *"This is the work of God, that ye believe on him whom he hath sent"* (John 6:29). What He most desires from you is not your hard work but your belief—your faith! Why? Because belief is what makes the gift yours.

My grandkids seem to get past these two decisions quickly on Christmas and birthdays. They don't usually have much trouble believing and receiving.

Chapter Ten—Believing on Christ

Yet, so many people I meet can't seem to do this with God. So, how about you, right now? Is this really something that you need to contemplate fifty-seven ways? Is this really something you need to find eighty-two reasons not to accept? It's a gift of God. It's free for the taking. If you believe the words of Jesus, if you will take God at His word, this can be yours right now.

Here's how God describes the taking of the gift:

> *That if thou shalt confess with thy mouth the Lord Jesus, and shalt believe in thine heart that God hath raised him from the dead, thou shalt be saved. For with the heart man believeth unto righteousness; and with the mouth confession is made unto salvation.*—Romans 10:9–10

Did you catch that? *"For with the heart man believeth unto righteousness..."*—that's the **believe** part. *"And with the mouth confession is made unto salvation"* —that's the **receive** part.

Again, in verse 13 He says, *"For whosoever shall call upon the name of the Lord shall be saved."* In other words, whoever will ask can have this gift from God.

In Acts 16:31 we are instructed, *"Believe on the Lord Jesus Christ, and thou shalt be saved."*

Once again in John 3:16 Jesus said, *"For God so loved the world, that he gave his only begotten Son, that whosoever believeth in him should not perish, but have everlasting life."*

Many times God says that this gift becomes ours by believing and receiving. It starts internally—in the heart. It starts with authentic or sincere belief—faith.

Friend, it's important that you realize there are two kinds of belief. There is a "head belief" and a "heart belief." A head belief is simply a knowledge of something. A heart belief is actually trusting that knowledge. We could call this "core belief" versus "mental assent."

If I went to LAX airport and bought a ticket on Southwest Airlines to Phoenix, I could believe in my head that this ticket and this airline could take me to Phoenix. I could know this in my head without actually placing my core trust in this airplane, this airline, this pilot, etc. This is head belief or "mental assent."

Heart belief would be to actually get on board the plane—to fully trust that airline and airplane to take me to my destination. This is the difference between mentally affirming a reality versus placing my core trust in that reality.

Chapter Ten—Believing on Christ

You may already have a head belief or mental knowledge of Jesus. You may intellectually understand everything I've written about in this little book. Millions of people in the world claim to believe in Jesus, yet they go about day to day still attempting to pay for their own sins and refusing to simply admit their desperate state and fully trust His finished payment on the cross.

Has this ever moved from your head to your heart?

Has this ever become personal?

Sure, Jesus is "the Savior," but have you ever placed your core trust in Him as your *personal* Saviour?

The question now is this: Will you place a *heart belief* in Jesus Christ alone?

Are you willing to believe that nothing else and no one else can save you except Him?

Are you willing to turn fully to Jesus from a sincere heart of repentance and faith?

Will you truly believe to the point of fully trusting in only Jesus to save you and pay your sin debt?

What if you were trapped on the fifth floor of a burning building? Imagine you're hanging out a window, clinging to the building for dear life. You're holding tight to the building—and you're doomed.

Suddenly, the fire department sees you, spreads a net for you, and ten firemen begin yelling for you to jump into their net.

In that moment, you cannot trust both the net *and* the building. If you try to trust both, you'll die. You must make a 100% choice either way. If you trust the building, it will soon fall and engulf you in flames. Yet, to trust the firemen, you would have to let go of the building and jump by faith into the net. You would need to have more than a head belief. Intellect could tell you that the science works—the physics, the net, the firemen will save you. But your *jump* necessitates a heart belief—a 100% trust in the firemen. This is core trust.

In the moment you jump, you've made two split-second decisions. Do I believe these firemen? Will I receive their offer? If the answer to both questions is *yes*, then the jump is inevitable. In jumping you receive the firemen's offer of salvation.

It's so simple. So many religions and systems complicate this matter—they make it so DO-oriented. Many people are trying to cling to the building and believe the firemen at the same time.

You cannot trust DO and DONE at the same time.

Chapter Ten—Believing on Christ

You must now choose one or the other. You must make your choice about God's gift. If it's a gift, then it cannot be earned. If you must earn it, then it isn't a gift. Yet God says repeatedly that you cannot earn it and that it is indeed a gift.

Who do you believe, God or religion?

Your own opinion or God's word?

Back to those two choices—Do I believe God? Will I receive His gift?

How about it?

Do you believe the message of God to you? Do you believe in your heart that Jesus Christ is God? Do you believe that, despite your good points, you are still sinful and need a "rebuilding" miracle? Do you believe that Jesus paid for your sin and rose again from the dead? If you truly believe these things in your heart, then tell Him!

Receive the gift.

Hopefully, right now you're saying, "YES, YES, YES—who wouldn't?!"

God makes this very simple, *"For whosoever shall call upon the name of the Lord shall be saved"* (Romans 10:13). Since you can't physically walk up to God and take eternal life, He simply says, "Ask." Your heart's belief produces an honest confession to God.

Your internal decision to fully trust compels an external cry from the heart—the decision to receive (to ask for it). Believe, receive, and the gift is YOURS instantly!

DONE!

You're not DOING for this gift—you're deciding. You're simply making a choice to fully believe what has already been DONE.

So here's the purpose of these pages—the most important question you will ever read in your entire life. It determines where you will spend all of eternity.

Will you, in this moment, decide to believe and receive God's gift?

I'm assuming you're ready to tear into this gift as soon as you can get it with the hands of your heart!

Maybe you've already made this decision as you're reading. Maybe you have never prayed and aren't sure how to verbalize these things to God. That's okay. Maybe this will help.

If you have already internally made the "believe" decision, then I invite you to pray a simple, sincere prayer. Talk to Jesus. He's right there with you. He's real. He's very relatable. In fact, He's the one that has been working on your heart this whole time you've been reading. You don't have to use my words. It's not a magic prayer, I'm just trying to help. Put it into your

Chapter Ten—Believing on Christ

own words if you want to, but talk to Him. He's the Hero who is saving you, and His is the love you've been looking for your whole life.

Maybe say something like this to Him right now:

Jesus,

I believe in my heart that you are God. I believe that you died for all my sins and rose again. I confess to you that I am a sinner, and I ask you to be my personal Savior right now. I place 100% of my core trust in you. Come into my life, give me your life, and take me to Heaven to be with you someday. I accept your free gift of eternal life.

Thank you for keeping your promise and answering this prayer.

Amen.

Did you believe and receive? If not, I hope you will very soon. Don't risk another day. God invites you to make this decision now, and He is eager for you to accept His gift. He says, *"Behold, now is the accepted time; behold, now is the day of salvation"* (2 Corinthians 6:2).

His rescue mission is complete, but you must choose to be rescued.

If you just placed your core trust in Jesus—congratulations on the greatest decision you will ever make! In His mercy and grace, God has applied the full payment of Jesus Christ for your sin debt to your account. The record is wiped clean forever, and you are perfect, righteous, and justified (just as if you'd never sinned) in God's sight!

This doesn't mean you won't still sin. In fact, you will—but when you do, you already have forgiveness, and the price for that sin has already been paid.

You are now "born again." Jesus Christ has come into your life to stay, and He has begun the process of growing you in His grace. He has rebuilt you spiritually from the ground up. You may not feel different, but according to God's own words you are a "new creature" with Jesus Christ living inside of you. You literally have a new set of spiritual genes (a new nature), your old sin nature is crucified (Romans 6:6), and the life of Christ is now within you.

You will never face eternity apart from God. You never need to fear His wrath or condemnation because His perfect love casts away all fear (1 John 4:18). He promises you eternal life which can never be taken away under any circumstance (Romans 8:35–39). You never again need to fear death or wonder where you

Chapter Ten—Believing on Christ

will go after you die. You have accepted what Christ has DONE for you. You didn't DO anything to earn it, and you can't DO anything to lose it.

You now belong to God, and He is your heavenly Father forever.

I told you we would get back to this verse, *"And you hath he quickened, who were dead in trespasses and sins"* (Ephesians 2:1). *Quickened* means "made alive"! God has brought you to life, spiritually speaking!

What a great decision. What a great future you have. A wonderful new life has been planted in you!

There are a few more things you really should know before you put this book down.

CONCLUSION

New Creature, New Life, New Future

Remember how I said we don't need a mere makeover, but we do need a total spiritual rebuild? Jesus called it "rebirth."

Well, that's what just happened to you!

You were born into God's family. You were "made alive" to God, and with this new birth comes some important things. God says you are literally a new creature. Second Corinthians 5:17 says, *"Therefore if any man be in Christ, he is a new creature: old things are passed away; behold, all things are become new."*

You are now alive in God's sight—whereas before you were spiritually dead. This means you have the capacity, by God's grace in your heart, to experience a personal relationship with Jesus daily. This is the close relationship He has always wanted with you, and it will lead to all kinds of internal changes (for the better) in your life! You now have the capacity to truly change for the better by God's power. God will grow you and change you from within if you will let Him.

God instructs us in 1 Peter 2:2, *"As newborn babes, desire the sincere milk of the word, that ye may grow thereby."* In God's family, you are a newborn babe! You have a new beginning in God's sight, and there's much growth to experience in your new life.

You have been "born again" the Bible way—God's way, just as 1 Peter 1:23 says, *"Being born again, not of corruptible seed, but of incorruptible, by the word of God, which liveth and abideth for ever."*

As we close this book and rejoice in your decision to accept God's gift, there are a few things you need to know.

First, you can never lose your salvation! You are secure in God's care forever. Though there are many, here are a couple of references that tell us this in the Bible:

Conclusion—New Creature, New Life, New Future

> *For I am persuaded, that neither death, nor life, nor angels, nor principalities, nor powers, nor things present, nor things to come, Nor height, nor depth, nor any other creature, shall be able to separate us from the love of God, which is in Christ Jesus our Lord.*—Romans 8:38–39

> *In whom ye also trusted, after that ye heard the word of truth, the gospel of your salvation: in whom also after that ye believed, ye were sealed with that holy Spirit of promise.*
> —Ephesians 1:13

This verse in Ephesians teaches that God sealed you (permanently placed His seal of ownership upon you) the moment you accepted Christ.

Again God promises in Hebrews 13:5, *"I will never leave thee, nor forsake thee."*

These are just a few of God's promises that once you have been "born" into His family, you can never be "unborn"!

Second, God wants you to grow as a newborn child. As a newborn baby has much to learn about life, so is your relationship with God. He says in 2 Peter 3:18, *"But grow in grace, and in the knowledge of our Lord and Saviour Jesus Christ. To him be glory both now and for ever. Amen."*

There are many ways you can grow closer to God. In Acts 2, the people who trusted Christ gathered together at church to learn the Bible, celebrate Jesus (God calls it worship), and encourage each other. It's important that you soon find a true Bible-believing and Bible-teaching church where each week you can learn more about Jesus and find friends who will encourage you in your journey.

If you allow me, there are some ways I would love to help you on the journey.

My books *Real Christianity* and *Stop Trying* were written to be your next steps. The first unpacks how to enjoy a real relationship with Jesus. You haven't joined a religion, you have met a person! The adventure of knowing Him, loving Him, enjoying Him, and letting Him guide and teach you every day forward has just begun. The second book unpacks who Jesus says you are and how your new identity changes the way you go at life from your core motivations. Visit Amazon.com soon to grab a copy of *Real Christianity* or *Stop Trying*.

I also host a YouTube channel designed for your spiritual formation—*Growing in the Gospel with Cary*

Conclusion—New Creature, New Life, New Future

Schmidt. On the channel, you will find daily devotional videos and a host of playlists featuring important Bible teaching series for your spiritual growth. It's all there for your blessing, so dive in!

Finally, for more copies of this little book, visit IntheGospel.com or Amazon.com. At In the Gospel, you will find free digital versions of *Done* in many different languages so you can share this good news with those you love and care for.

More than a million copies of *Done* have been distributed, and every week someone emails me to tell me they received Jesus as their personal Savior. I would love to receive an email from you!

If you contact us, we will also try to recommend a good church in your area where you can learn the Bible and grow in God's grace with a healthy Christian family.

You have a new life! You are a new creature in God's sight! You have a new eternal destiny and a new heavenly Father! He wants to provide your every need, guide your every decision, transform your life from the inside out, and lead you into a future that fulfills His eternal purpose.

Just as you trust Him by faith for salvation, He wants you to grow in faith day by day—learning more of His love, His Word, and His plan for your life.

You're going to love the journey of growing closer to God. Now that your sin debt is taken care of, you have an invitation to enter His presence at any moment. Hebrews 4:16 says, *"Let us therefore come boldly unto the throne of grace, that we may obtain mercy, and find grace to help in time of need."*

You don't need a priest or a mediator—you can come directly to your heavenly Father at any time. You can talk with Him through prayer, and He will talk with you through His word, the Bible. He says that His word is *"quick, and powerful, and sharper than any twoedged sword, piercing even to the dividing asunder of soul and spirit, and of the joints and marrow, and is a discerner of the thoughts and intents of the heart"* (Hebrews 4:12).

I encourage you to begin reading the word of God and begin praying to Him every day. You'll find day by day that your heart will desire to grow closer and closer to Him. The more you get to know Jesus, the more you will love Him! The more you find out how much He loves you and just what He has done for you, the more irresistible you will find Him!

We began our journey with this verse:

> *Come now, and let us reason together, saith the*
> *LORD: though your sins be as scarlet, they shall*

Conclusion—New Creature, New Life, New Future

be as white as snow; though they be red like crimson, they shall be as wool. —Isaiah 1:18

You have accepted God's gift—Jesus Christ. He has taken away your sin. As a result, you have become a new creature in His sight—not by what you DO, but by what He has DONE.

Congratulations on your entrance into the family of God. You never need to fear death again. You forever have the promise of eternal life—not because you earned it, but because you accepted God's gift.

Now, you hold the greatest and most important message ever given by God to mankind.

Who do you know that needs to hear this message?

Would you share it with them? Would you pass a copy of this book on to them? Go now and let someone else know it's not about DO…

It's about DONE!

Now begin to let Jesus transform your life from the inside out. Let His goodness within show itself through your good life. *"For we are his workmanship, created in Christ Jesus unto good works, which God hath before ordained that we should walk in them"* (Ephesians 2:10). Live for Jesus, not to *earn* His favor, but *because it is already yours!*

Done

Look forward to your future with great confidence and expectation!

> *But as it is written, Eye hath not seen, nor ear heard, neither have entered into the heart of man, the things which God hath prepared for them that love him.* —1 Corinthians 2:9

May God bless you as you begin your new life in Jesus Christ! He will never let you down!

Thanks for reading!

Have you trusted Christ as your personal Savior as a result of this book? If so, please contact us as soon as possible so we can rejoice in your decision and send you tools for growth in your new relationship with God.

✉	**WRITE**	2875 W Ray Rd Suite 6-346 Chandler, AZ 85224
☎	**CALL**	(888) 405-6326
⌨	**EMAIL**	done@inthegospel.com
🖱	**GO ONLINE**	shop.inthegospel.com

About the Author

Cary Schmidt (M.Min., D.Min.) serves as the senior pastor of Emmanuel Baptist Church in Newington, Connecticut. He and his wife, Dana, have been blessed with three children, their spouses, and five grandchildren, and they have enjoyed over thirty years of marriage and ministry together. Cary's passion is to love God, love his family and church family, develop spiritual leaders, and point people to Jesus Christ through leading, teaching, and writing. He has authored more than a dozen books and hosts the Growing in the Gospel YouTube Channel and the Leading in the Gospel podcast. You can connect with Cary at caryschmidt.com.

Also available from Cary Schmidt

Real Christianity

Are you enjoying your Christian life? Or are you exhausted with trying? Do you understand how your Christian life works? Or are you frustrated with failure? Are you interested in real Christianity? Or are you held hostage by religious tradition?

In this compelling book, Cary Schmidt candidly and simply unpacks what real Christianity is all about. Through these pages, learn how you can embrace the grace, endure the struggle, and enjoy the relationship of truly knowing Jesus! (240 pages, paperback)

Also available from Cary Schmidt

Stop Trying

From looking outwardly to please others to looking inwardly to define ourselves, we constantly try to cultivate or construct our identities. But guided by the whims of culture or the faulty advice of tradition, we often find identity collapses when life falls apart or change threatens that fragile structure.

In *Stop Trying*, Cary Schmidt's storytelling creates compelling scenes in which you'll see yourself and your *self*. You'll understand why defining your identity outside of Jesus Christ is ultimately fragile, hollow, and unsatisfying. And you'll discover that your truest and most fulfilling identity is a byproduct of a relationship that changes everything. (240 pages, paperback)

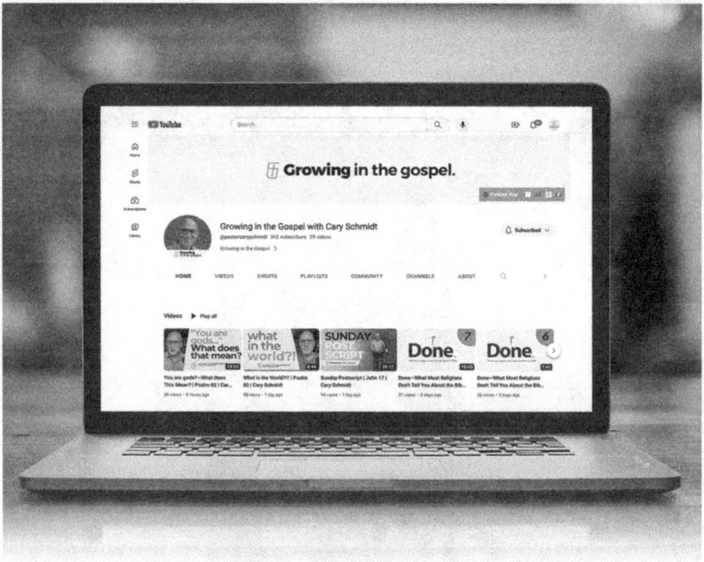

Growing in the gospel.

Daily devotions with encouraging biblical teaching

Follow and Subscribe at
youtube.com/@pastorcaryschmidt